# Beautiful Mess

Melissa Marti

Trilogy Christian Publishers
A Wholly Owned Subsidiary of Trinity Broadcasting Network
2442 Michelle Drive
Tustin, CA 92780

For information, address Trilogy Christian Publishing
Rights Department, 2442 Michelle Drive, Tustin, Ca 92780.
Trilogy Christian Publishing/ TBN and colophon are trademarks of Trinity Broadcasting Network.

For information about special discounts for bulk purchases, please contact Trilogy Christian Publishing.

Manufactured in the United States of America

10 9 8 7 6 5 4 3 2 1

Library of Congress Cataloging-in-Publication Data is available.

ISBN 978-1-64088-977-4 (Print Book)
ISBN 978-1-64088-978-1 (ebook)

To the younger, broken Melissa who thought she had no value or worth but somehow found a way to keep going and not give up.

To those who are out there now struggling with similar hurts and fears—you are not alone.

But most of all, to the man who stuck with me when it would have been much easier to leave. You have my heart always. You never let me off the hook when I acted like a fool, but you were steadfast in your caring for me. You were my constant, "continuously present over a period of time." You never changed, always remained the same. I would not be me without you.

# CONTENTS

# INTRODUCTION

MANY OF US HAVE SPENT much of our time in life questioning our value. We let the circumstances that surround our life define who we are. But it is *not* who we are—it is simply what we have lived through. And the amazing thing about it is we *did* live through it. We may have fallen. We may have scars and mine may look different than yours, but we all have them. Some of these may be because of our choices and some could be from things beyond our control. Regardless, we are still here. Not only did we survive but also we can actually thrive (defined as to prosper or flourish) because of what we have experienced.

Beyond these pages are my story. Be prepared. The stories are real, the feelings even more so. I will try to share as transparently as possible. I will protect the identity of all. I am not sharing this for sympathy as I am not a victim anymore. The stories are to inspire your faith, to encourage your heart, and to challenge you to believe in who you are. *You* are not your circumstances. You are not what others say or believe about you. The only person you are is who you choose to believe you are—actually, more than even who you believe you are—because fortunately for us, we have One who always believes in us even when we don't believe in ourselves.

I am so thankful for the never-ending love, grace, and strength our Lord God gives us even when we don't seek it. This is a story of triumph, a story of a life that from the beginning was unplanned and even unwanted but has become a testimony of God's never-ending faithfulness. It is a story of seeing past the external to the core of who I really am. It is a story of seeing past the moments of pain and understanding the eternal value of me, my life, my purpose.

# CHAPTER 1

## What Is in a Name?

I'm Melissa Michelle Brophy, born in November 14 at 1:04 p.m., at Bryan Memorial Hospital, Lincoln, Nebraska, to Mary Collins and Doug Marti. What? Brophy, Collins, Marti? How? What is the rhyme or reason to this? It makes no sense.

This is what my birth certificate reads. And for most of my life, it broke my heart. You see, I was born to two people who were not married and did not expect my coming. I am not unlike many people in that regard. What sets me apart is the story after.

My parents had a true love story. What makes a good love story but forbidden love and tragedy? My father was twenty years older than my mom. His oldest daughter was a mere two weeks younger than her. This created a terrible situation for all involved. There was much anger, bitterness, and striving, so much so that when I was only two and a half years old, my father decided he couldn't be the father or husband he expected of himself and he took his life on Father's Day weekend. He made his statement. He wrote three different suicide notes—one for me, one for his other children, and one for my mom. He stated how he failed at being a good father, good husband, and good lawyer and we would all be better off without him.

In his note to me, he wrote, "To my beautiful Melissa"; he expressed his sorrow for not being the person I needed him to be and that he couldn't go on anymore. I knew I was the cause for the heartache. I knew he couldn't choose between myself and my mom or his four children. I knew he chose to give up rather than live. I carried the guilt of this for a very long time. I often wondered why I was born—just to cause my dad to die? The weight of all of it was a huge struggle. I couldn't share it with anyone since they just would not understand. So instead I just internalized it and began to slowly hate myself and everything I represented.

I was never given his name because I was born out of wedlock and he never finished the process of changing it. When he died, I was known as the bastard of the family. It was questioned if I should even receive my inheritance and definitely could *not* have his name. My mom was from the wrong side of the tracks, considered white trash compared to the Marti family who had a lineage of political presence and wealth. There was no way I would be allowed to be considered family. This would tarnish the Marti name for sure.

My family turned their back on me. I was only two. I had no control over my circumstances or how I was conceived, but they were bound to define me. The rest of my life was a struggle for me and my identity. I wanted to be accepted, loved, and just acknowledged. I craved it and did everything in my young mind to make it happen. My mom suffered in her own way. She just disappeared. I felt like she couldn't bear the sight of me because of my father's death. I spent much of my time with my grandma, aunts, and step-dad. I was shuffled from here to there and was an inconvenience to almost everyone in my life.

I sought to prove everyone wrong, to show them I had value. I was the perfect student. I was the people-pleaser to my friends. I sought to find my identity in anything or anyone who would give it to me. Nothing ever filled the void in my heart. When I was only thirteen years old, I would fantasize about what it would be like for everyone if I died too, how much better their lives would be. I looked at the pills in the medicine cabinet, but there's nothing there other than Tylenol or ibuprofen. I thought about other ways, but nothing seemed to be realistic, so I eventually grew weary and gave up. I saw myself as a failure at even that.

About that time, my grandfather, my dad's dad, decided to enter my life. We spent quite a bit of time together, and I fell in love with him. He was strong and opinionated, but under the gruff exterior, I knew he loved me back. He was everything I needed. He would tell me stories of my dad and I finally felt like I belonged. But my siblings on that side of the family became aware of what was going on and became upset. They felt betrayed by him and he distanced himself. Once again, someone had to choose between me and someone else. I lost out. For the life of me, I could not understand what was so vile about me, why I couldn't be loved. I had done nothing to anyone. I had never caused pain intentionally, but it seemed my mere life caused everyone I met sorrow. I was devastated. I just for once wanted to be chosen.

I became very involved in church. I loved God with my whole heart. And I found a peace I had never known. I remember one summer at camp, the preacher said, "God is like your earthly father." *What?* No! I couldn't handle that. The only example I had of an earthly father was my dad, who took his life over being there for me and my stepdad who struggled with alcohol. The vision of God in my head was someone who would kick me when I was down and then leave me to survive on my own. I cried unconsolably at that. I knew if I wasn't perfect in every way, I would be abandoned. I couldn't go through that again.

Children look to their fathers for their identity. I had no one to look to. I was confused and alone and heartbroken. I eventually quit trying. I quit school my senior year. I was ranked eighth in a class of 856 students. I had skipped a grade and was top of my class. But none of that mattered. My heart could not take the feeling of rejection and abandonment any longer. I had been to ten elementary schools and six high schools and I did not "fit in" anywhere. I was only seventeen years old. I had given up on life.

I went off to college, though I only stayed for a semester and left. I took a job as a nanny in New York City and became anorexic. I figured I could slowly kill myself. It didn't matter anyway. Everyone would be happier if I was gone. Their lives would be better. There was nothing that I could do that would take away the pain and the sorrow I had in my heart. I took up drinking. I was a terrible drunk. I was so angry and sad that I became reckless and almost challenged God. I would yell at Him. I would even curse Him for being born. What was the point? Just to live in torture and pain?

Finally, one night, in April of 1993, I went out with some of my friends. I gave away all my valuable things and planned that this would be the night. It would all end and I could be put out of my suffering and isolation. You see, even though I had people around me, I still felt horribly alone. No one knew the depths of despair I had lived in all these years. I kept it hidden because how could anyone even think of loving me if they knew? I wanted so badly to be loved, to be accepted, to be valued, to be seen, and to be chosen. Yet I never was. I was the source of pain, the object of ridicule, the one overlooked and left behind. It was just too much and had gone on too long.

We got to the dance hall and I had consumed two bottles of wine on a completely empty stomach. I hadn't eaten anything in weeks. I ran in to an ex-boyfriend who humiliated me in front of my friends, and I lost it. I ran from the building and sat down in the middle of the highway. I wasn't moving. A car started coming down the road at fifty-five miles an hour. I wasn't moving. I could read the numbers on the tag because it got so close. I closed my eyes expecting it to hit me and end all my pain.

But it did not. Instead a man, about seven feet tall, came from out of nowhere and scooped me up and threw me on the side of the road safely away from the car. My friends witnessed this. When I looked up, he simply disappeared into nothingness. I believe he was an angel. I began to shake. My friends ran to where I was, and they picked me up and put me in the car. I could not stop shaking. Maybe it was partly all the alcohol I consumed, but mostly because of the event that had just occurred.

As we drove, I had a vision. I saw myself being pulled by my ankles down by demonic forces, and I saw God's hand reach down and I heard the audible voice of Him saying, "No! She is *mine.*" I wept. I knew that God had intervened in my life. He said I was *His.* No one had ever said that. My friends had seen the event (not the vision) and could not stop talking about the "man." It forever changed the trajectory of my life.

I still had feelings of self-doubt and even self-hate, but I was moved to seek why God had chosen to spare my life. Was there a purpose after all? If so, what was it? I began asking questions of God. I began putting fleeces before Him for direction. I eventually ended up in Alabama working as an intern in a campus ministry program. It was during that time that God gave me a scripture—Psalms 45:16 says, "Your sons will take the place of your fathers; you will make them princes throughout the land." He went on to tell me that my grandfather was going to pass away and to be prepared.

Two weeks later, I got the call that he had died. My heart broke. He was the only man in my entire life who had loved me. I boarded a plane and went back home for the funeral. I was not greeted warmly at all. In fact, my eldest brother said to me, "You will not speak, you will be seen and not heard, and you are not allowed to sit with the family or you will be removed by security."

I looked at him with tears in my eyes and simply said, "I am not here for you or anyone else. I am here for Grandpa." I went to the very back of the auditorium holding my head as high as I possibly could knowing I was again not wanted or accepted.

What followed was even more heartbreaking. I know now why God had said to prepare myself. My grandfather had prepared a will of course and I was part of it. I was actually the subject of most of it. He specifically wrote, "Melissa Michelle Brophy, your sister, and Doug's daughter." I wept. I had been acknowledged! I was not forgotten. I did not want anything else from him, not his money or his property or anything tangible. I had gotten the best inheritance I could receive—to be seen as a part of the family. But my siblings were not ready for that. So, in an effort to keep the peace, I signed away any rights I had and went back to Alabama. It was enough for me.

But God wasn't done with me or my siblings yet. I continued to pray and hope and believe for things to change. I got married and then divorced and took back my maiden name. And one day in September of 2016 (twenty-three years later), I was sitting in the McDonald's drive-through when I got a Facebook message. It read, "Melissa, this is your sister. It has only taken me thirty years, but I want to know you." I wept. I could hardly believe it was true. My whole life, I had wanted relationship. And here it was staring me in the face. We met up and eventually I met my brother too. I fell in love with them. And for my birthday in 2017, they both said to me they wanted me to take the Marti name.

What is in a name? Does your name define you? No, it does not. But a name does represent who you belong to. When I finally let go and allowed God to be *who* I belonged to, when I became only concerned with being acknowledged by Him, that is when I found peace. I didn't seek the validation of man. It wasn't always easy. It was very lonely at times. But I did not give up. I trusted Him, and I never in a million years would have imagined two of my siblings would change their heart toward me and not only accept me but also invite me into their lives. God was my identity. Man was not. And when my heart got that revelation, He was able to move on my behalf to show me His love and acceptance of me. He was always there. In every situation of fear and rejection and abandonment, He was always present. I was never alone.

# CHAPTER 2

## *Addictions*

ADDICTION IS DEFINED AS "THE condition of exhibiting a compulsive, chronic, physiological, or psychological need for a habit-forming substance, thing, or activity." I am a child of an addict, a spouse of an addict, and struggled myself with addiction. My biological father was an alcoholic. My step-father was as well. I married a man who was a sex addict. And my addiction was with food. It was my comfort, my feel good.

Addictions are plain and simple a distraction from what hurts our heart and soul. Alcohol numbs the pain, causes us to lose our inhibitions, and for a moment maybe even relax and enjoy life. Food is a comfort. It fills our belly when what we really want is to fill our empty lonely heart. Sex for many is a temporary feeling of acceptance. It is exhilarating and can be addicting. But all these actions end up costing us in the end. The temporary fulfillment leaves us wanting more and more until it consumes us.

Alcohol affects our judgment. When my dad took his life, he had plenty of vodka and I think a little valium. All he wanted was for the pain to go away. He never considered how much pain he would leave for those left behind. He couldn't consider anything past the very moment he was in. But there is a ripple effect for every decision we make, whether we see it or not. And addictions are passed down in families. They may manifest in different ways, but they are there.

My mom's addiction to money and things caused her to spend too much and aggravate the relationship she had with my stepdad who struggled with alcohol as well. When we are in despair and disappointment, we tend to react in ways that cause more pain. We do not mean to hurt others. There is a saying "hurt people hurt people" (usually unintentionally). It is very true. I grew up in much turmoil in our home. I would come home from school and a moving truck would be in our driveway. It was time to move on again. The cycle of arguing and anger and violence was never-ending in my life. I would stay in shelters just to sleep in peace. I remember one shelter there was a teenage girl who lived there with her family. When I watched her boyfriend drop her off, in my heart, I longed for the normalcy of her life—simple, peace, love, and acceptance.

I met my husband in Alabama when I was interning with the campus ministry group. He was in the army and stationed in Georgia. He was charismatic and handsome and so full of confidence. His smile and charm won me over. We dated for six months and then got engaged. My pastors recommended we seek premarital counseling and take things slow. But I had finally met the one who I thought had chosen me. I couldn't risk losing it by taking too long to marry. Besides, did the past really matter? All that mattered was that we wanted to be together. We did not listen to those that God had placed in our life and ran off and eloped just one month after getting engaged. The words of my close friend and roommate echoed in my mind, "You are going to just give up your dream to minister and follow him around the country?"

I replied, "He is my dream and I will give up what I have to in order to have him."

I finally had it all! Just four months after we got married, we found out we were pregnant. I couldn't have been happier. My dream, to be a mom and a wife, was coming to be. And it was a girl! My heart swelled with love and pride. I had finally gotten it altogether. My fairy tale was here, and I was living it. My first child Meg was born in 1995. I was so in love, not only with her but also with my husband and my life. I could not ask for more.

In the spring of 1996, the Olympics came to Atlanta and my husband got orders to go. It wasn't terribly far from where we were stationed, but I had a new baby and he became enamored with the "college life" he had never experienced. We grew apart. I was insecure and he was irritated. But that fall he came home, and we began our lives together again. Our relationship was strained. I reached out to him but he was very distant. I desperately wanted to reconcile, and I tried everything to win his heart back.

One day while cleaning out the car, I found a notepad and I opened it up. The first thing I read was, "To my Dear Amy." The note went on to declare his love and affection for this person. My heart sunk. I couldn't breathe or swallow. My world spun out of control. I was staring at the proof that the love of my life had chosen another woman. We hadn't been married two years and I couldn't keep his love that long. I became angry. I confronted him with his words. I told him I wasn't making it easy on him or her and I was not giving up!

He cried and apologized and professed his love for me. We decided to muddle through. We were both broken. This became the cycle of my life for the next seventeen years. My husband was a sex addict. He had many affairs, and with each affair, he became even angrier. While we enjoy our addictions, we don't always want the consequences that go along with them. We try to compartmentalize and we think one thing won't affect another, but that simply is not true. So the very thing I was trying to escape by marrying him I was now living out. Sure, it wasn't alcohol, but it was much worse.

His addictions caused me to question my value. The issues of pornography and other women were more than I could bear. But we had children and I could not let them down. I questioned my worth. Once again, I struggled with my identity. The enemy knows our weakness. He doesn't play fair. I hoped and prayed and believed if I did everything right, my husband would see my love for him—my sacrificial love putting him and his needs first, that he would fall in love with me again and walk away from the addictions, that he would choose me over the temporary satisfaction that drew him away so easily. But it was not meant to be.

This became increasingly clear with the final straw being one night when I called the school he was attending to discuss our oldest daughter's account (she was enrolled in college while still in high school). I asked them if we could discuss his account to which they informed me he was no longer a student there. What? He had been "going to class" every Tuesday and Thursday night for months now. How could he not be a student? My heart sank to the pit of my stomach, and all this took place right in front of our daughter. She heard. She knew. Again, she looked me in the face and asked frankly, "How many times are you going to do this to yourself, Mom?"

I was left to make a decision. Either I could keep going in the marriage and lose very part of who I was or I could pick myself up and move on alone. I chose the harder one.

I still loved my husband. I knew I could not live with lies, deceit, and other women any longer. He cried. He asked me to give yet another chance. You see, I believe he truly loved me. Addiction is a terrible mistress; it will cost you everything. It cost us our marriage. Our love story was over. I told him I would spend my whole life thinking he was lying, and he would spend his trying to prove otherwise and it wasn't fair to either one of us.

I did not get away unscathed. I too had an addiction. Mine became food, the control of it. I would vacillate between not eating at all and eating everything I could to fill the void in my soul. I was battling the voices of my past—"You are fat and ugly. No one will ever love you." They were screaming. I could do nothing to silence them as much as I tried. So for a while, I gave in to them. I became a prisoner to food and my body image.

We divorced after almost nineteen years of marriage and five children. My dreams were shattered. I saw myself as a failure in every aspect, just as my father had his life. But unlike my father, I had God. While things were extremely painful and lonely, and my life was totally upside down, I still had a small shred of hope. I had enough fight in me to not give in to the addictions of my life or my husband's life. I remembered the night I tried to end my life and I heard again, "No, she is *mine*." I belonged, not to a man but to my God. I had a purpose. I was given five beautiful precious lives. How could I ask for more than that? The love from those sweet souls could never be matched. They were my gift. I had to break the cycle of addiction, fear, self-doubt, and self-hate. My purpose? Well, it became clear, love. Love in spite of it all. Love despite the pain.

I took some time to mourn, to grieve, the loss of my dream so I could let God show me a new dream. I let go of what I thought I wanted so He could show me His plan. It took time. It took being intentional and not giving up. It took letting God fill the void in my heart and not trying to fill it myself. It was a process and did not happen overnight and was not always fun. But I can tell you this, being where I am today is much more fulfilling than anything I have known.

# CHAPTER 3

## *Fear*

FEAR CAUSES US TO ACT in ways that contradict what we know to be right—fear of being alone, fear of failure, or fear of any kind. Not waiting and being patient and walking in faith will end up causing more pain than just allowing God the freedom to work His plan in our lives. My biggest fear is being alone.

I went four years after my divorce without dating. I watched my friends live happy lives with another. I even introduced my best friend to her now husband and best friend. I sat by and watched and waited and wondered. I tried to stay busy and not think about what I was missing in my life. I quieted the voices that said, "No one will ever love you."

I stayed busy with work and traveled. Then I wouldn't have time to think about it. But the company I worked for went under, and I had to find a new job. I took one at my church. I felt being surrounded by people who loved God would be healing for me. And it was. I made some incredible friends and became a part of the women's and men's ministry. I joined the prayer team and even a Bible study. It was there that I met someone. He was our small group leader. He was in men's ministry and on the altar team. I found him incredibly handsome and charming.

I learned he was a writer and we began to share stories, scriptures, worship songs, and essentially our hearts. Not a day would go by without a word of encouragement or expression of love between us. He even sent me prayers. Our first date was a worship concert, and I felt that I had finally found the one God had meant for me to live the rest of my life with.

After a month of dating, he asked to talk to me and said he wanted to share something with me that could affect our relationship. I listened to him share a very personal issue he said he struggled with back in college. I said that I did not care, that it was a long time ago, and that people all have things in the past that does not define who we are today. He seemed relieved and began to be more at ease with me. The longer we dated, the harder it was to not have any physical contact. As much as I wanted to stay pure and honor God, it became more and more difficult. What began as simple acts of love became much more. And as anyone knows, when you get too intimate, you become attached. It is the way God designed intimacy—it creates a bond.

I knew he had some identity issues and some things from his past that he struggled with, but I believed our love for each other and that God would cover all of that. Five months after we began dating, he proposed, and I said yes. We began planning our "second chapter" of life together. He had been married for almost twenty-three years, so he knew the pain and disappointment of a failed marriage. During our courtship, he exhibited signs of aggression and anger. He showed his ability to be emotionally abusive and manipulating, but I wanted to believe he just needed to experience unconditional love and he would come around. And he would always come back after an argument with words of love and affirmation. So, despite my friends and family warning me of their concerns, I went on to marry him. (Does this sound familiar?)

He called me "the one," and he said I was destined to be his forever. Forever only lasted nine months. My fear of being alone caused me to overlook red flags. It caused me to silence my loved ones' concerns and even ignore them. Fear led me down a very hard road—a road that devastated me more than the nineteen years of adultery and anger, a road where I questioned my worth like never before.

You see, his struggle was very personal. It was a war within himself of his very identity. When you do not know your own identity and question if you should be someone other than what God made you to be, you become angry and bitter. You attack those who are close to you. Because you are so unhappy with yourself, you cannot stand to see another succeed, so you tear them down. You try to bring them to your level. All the words of love and encouragement were gone. The tenderness was gone and all that was left were attacks and harsh tones.

I found out he had not been completely honest with me before we got married, and it put me in a very bad position. I had to deal with not only the deceit and hurt but also the possibility of health issues because of it. My head was spinning. My heart had been on an emotional roller coaster, and I was never sure if I was up or down or what was coming around the bend. It became too much for me to contain anymore.

One day, I was weeping and asked him, "Why? Why did you marry me? You used to be kind and now you are just mean." His response was, "I was wooing you. I don't have to do that anymore." I was devastated. He believed because I loved God and I believed in marriage, I would endure his abusive ways. Our private life was unbelievably painful and personally humiliating. But he kept telling me I was "the one." The one? The one for what? The one to take the brunt of your anger, your perversion, your demeaning words? No, I would not. I was past the fear of being alone, past the fear of judgment, past the fear of standing up for myself and its consequences.

So one Sunday morning while he was at church, I decided to not live in fear anymore. I decided to take back my life despite what the church would think. I moved out. I left him the wedding pictures, his desk, a futon to sleep on, and my lingerie in the closet. I faced a lot of questions from those who thought they knew him. I endured a lot of judgment and cried many tears. I was again alone, but being alone was far better than what I had lived those nine months. I would not let fear again rule my heart.

Fear is the opposite of faith and I know we have all heard it. But faith is having confidence of something, trust and belief in good. Faith brings peace. Fear is a belief that something is dangerous and likely to cause pain. If you are afraid of being alone because you think it will be painful, let me assure you my friend nothing is as painful as being with someone who disregards everything about you, whose only pleasure in life is to make you feel less than, to question your value and your worth.

I have learned the hard way that the only person in life who gets to define you is you and God, because His definition of you is perfect. He says, "I formed you in your mother's womb," and everything God does is perfect. He does not make mistakes. We make the mistake by putting Him in a box and expecting Him to act on our every desire. We think that just because things don't go exactly as we had envisioned, God is not for us. It simply is not true. Just as a parent knows what is best for their child and says no because they see the *whole* picture, so is God with us. He sees from beginning to end and we only see a small part. Fear causes us to doubt. Faith causes us to rest and believe. God can move mountains with faith because we are giving Him permission to do His will. Trust me, His will is always better than our desires.

# CHAPTER 4

## *Living for Today*

IT'S GOOD TO LEARN FROM things. It's healthy to remember events and moments of time. What is not fruitful is to live in the past or even in the future. Living in the past creates depression because we relive and critique and regret. Living in the future creates anxiety when we can't see things coming to pass in the way or time *we* think it should be.

When I first got divorced, it was such a strange thing to me. I didn't have anyone to plan my day for. There was no one to try and please. I had no one directing me on what I should be doing or their expectations of how my day should look. I had been trained to think of everyone before myself and do what their bidding was. It had become such a part of me I was simply void. I felt empty. I was lost. I would toss to and fro, making a decision and then questioning if it were really the right one.

I remember my first trip alone to Virginia. I was there for six months on a project manager job for our construction company doing fiber optic installation. I woke up the first day there (a few days early to get to know the area), and I almost had a panic attack trying to figure out if I should go eat breakfast, take a long walk downtown, go drive in the mountains, go shopping, or stay in and just rest and relax watching the football game on.

My whole life was built around someone else. It was fulfilling his dream by being everything he wanted. I still got to live my dream of having a family, being a wife and a mother, so I did not mind giving up what I considered the everyday events of life for the big picture of life I thought I possessed. But eventually I lost who I was created to be. Compromises are a good part in any relationship; it causes us to have balance and not be so self-centered. But in an unhealthy relationship, when you are constantly settling for less, it is very destructive. So when I finally took the leap to regain my life, I had *no* clue what I wanted or even what I was capable of attaining. I had no confidence in who I was or even in who God had created me to be. I questioned God. I felt let down, betrayed. I had this formula in my head if I did everything right, followed all the rules, then it would all work out. Foolishly, I thought my actions could influence another's to change. But God didn't want me focusing so much on my husband, almost making him an idol in my life. Yes, I needed to live in a way that would bring honor to both God and my husband, but I needed to make sure I was honoring myself as well, setting boundaries and fulfilling the purpose God gave me. I did not do that.

I became a prisoner to my own dream. I gave up who I was and who God called me to be. I do not believe God wants divorce for His children, but I do believe He wants what is best for us. And living in abuse is *not* His best. I believe he wanted more for me. He wanted me to have my dream because He is the one who gave it to me, but I needed to have it in a healthy way.

Just as we as parents will not allow our children certain things because we want what is best for them, God is a *good* father who will not allow us to hold onto things that will end up hurting us, regardless of how tightly we hold to them or cry for them or even throw a fit about them. He will calmly and patiently wait until we come to the end of ourselves and lovingly and graciously say no. And then we, as His children, have the opportunity to either submit and trust His way knowing His heart is toward us or to stubbornly refuse and thereby create more harm for ourselves.

I recently took a StrengthFinder test. My top 5 are as follows:

1. Belief
2. Responsibility
3. Consistency
4. Developer
5. Empathy

I learned that because of these strengths (which *God* gave me), belief and responsibility can come across as stubbornness. Belief drives me, because at my core being, I *know* that God is for me and that He created me to be a great wife and mother and encourager. I will not accept anything less. It drove me literally to pursue whatever means I could to make sure I lived out what I believed He had for me. But where I *failed* was in *trusting* Him to bring it to pass. I felt I needed to help, if you will, to pursue and overtake my dream. I was living in the future and not in the present. I was living out what I wanted and not what I actually had. What I thought I had and what was reality were not the same in any way, shape, or fashion. No matter how badly I wanted things to be different, I couldn't "will" them to change. It was out of my hands. So, when I lost the façade, I had no idea what to do with myself.

I began to look back at my choices. I began to relive my decisions. I began to question. I began to cry. I began to live in regret, which caused me to be sad, even depressed. I was angry at myself. Anger is a masked emotion. It covers what you are really feeling, either shame, disappointment, or fear. Mine was shame. I couldn't accept that my decisions had led me to the place I never wanted to be, *alone*. But it was truth. I had to look at my heart, my motives. I had to see myself in honesty and begin the process of healing.

As I started out on my own to begin my "new life," I had to learn to renew my mind. The patterns of thought had to change. I had lived so many years with certain thoughts that there became a "rut" in how I approached my life and situations and people. I would be going along doing well when all of a sudden, I would find I had diverted to my old way of thinking. I didn't trust people. I knew God loved me, but I felt no one in my life loved me. I felt unworthy, unacceptable. And I acted that way. I actually pushed people, tested them, and I expected to be rejected. I was so used to feeling that way that I created situations to live that out, over and over again. It was "safe," it was "normal," and it was comfortable. Why? Because it was all I had ever known. I was not God's best or His plan, but it was what I accepted as who I was. And God's desire was to remove that. He had to get me to a place on my own, *alone,* for me to see exactly how I was getting in the way of my own hopes and dreams. I finally gave in. I said, "Uncle," and decided to surrender.

I had to make a concerted effort every day to put on my "new mind." Romans 12:2 tells us, "Do not act like the sinful people of the world. Let God change your life. First of all, let Him give you a new mind. Then you will know what God wants you to do. And the things you do will be good and pleasing and perfect."

This is what I wanted! This is exactly what I was looking for, and by slowing down, letting my walls come down, and doing the very thing I dreaded most (being alone), I could quiet myself enough to hear the direction to walk.

Trust is a firm belief in the reliability, truth, ability, or strength of someone or something.

My strength—"belief"—is part of the definition of what God was putting as a deep, new path for me to walk in, trusting Him and knowing He will take care of me. I can live in today. I take every day as it comes, good or bad. I know that God is worthy of my belief in Him and His ability to care for me and bring my dreams to pass.

I found a freedom, one I had never experienced before. Freedom is quite simply being able to live at peace with who you really are. The problem I have found is most of us don't really know who we are. We know what we "are supposed" to be whether it be society, church, friends, or family and even work. But we do not know for ourselves who we really are.

Do we like hot or cold? Summer or winter? Coffee or soda? Or even deeper questions of, "What do I really want from my life?" Most of us settle. We find what is easy or acceptable and cease striving for what moves us, what makes our heart beat faster, or what gives us the motivation to go higher and farther than we ever imagined.

Some of us have had others make choices for us or have allowed them to be as I had in my marriage. We lose our voice and succumb to others' desires and give up who we really are inside or who we know we want to be. But when you break free from that, even for a moment, when you take the risk of stepping forward or backward and chance everything, then that is when you find yourself. That is when you begin living.

If you quiet the noise around you, and listen to your heart, and God's voice within you—yes, it is there—then you begin to believe in yourself. And when you believe in you, nothing can stop you! Think about when you finally make a decision and how fired up you get, how excited you feel, almost invincible. Take that and move forward. Do not look back. Don't allow yourself to be defeated. You only truly experience defeat if you give up.

# CHAPTER 5

## *Favor*

WHEN I GOT DIVORCED FROM my husband of nineteen years, I had been working for my church as their bookkeeper. I decided it was best for me to find a new job, a fresh start. So I went through a hiring agency and found a position with a start-up company that did work for telephone and Internet companies. The owner and I got to be good friends, and even though I only began as a bookkeeper, I quickly moved up in responsibility and took on project management.

It was an exciting time for me. I was able to travel, and I found a lot of self-worth in what I brought to the company. I was establishing a name for myself and doing things I never dreamed of. It was easy to get sucked into the adventure and lose the ability to make rational decisions.

One day, as my friend and I were talking, he mentioned taking out some loans for new trucks and machines necessary to expand the business. We had several contracts that promised a great income, so it sounded like a good idea. I was not an owner in the company, and he needed me to be so we could qualify for a loan. He put together paperwork that stated we were partners.

We proceeded to purchase four company trucks and a drilling machine with trailer and other smaller machines. I cosigned the loans with him, and they totaled roughly $300,000. I was a bit nervous about that much debt for me as I am a single mom of five, but he promised me that if anything went south, these would be taken care of before anything else. So we did it. We were partners, or so I thought.

My friend and partner was a good guy with terrible money skills. He spent much of our earnings before all the work was finalized and approved for quality assurance. As we got bigger, he decided to cut corners and keep the workforce small to keep more of the profit for himself. Our company had grossed over two million dollars, and we were a very small business. When the customer we were doing work for decided the quality was not up to par, they pulled the contract and all future income was gone. Not only was the income gone, but also the prepayment on work was being expected back. The company was in a lot of trouble.

We hobbled along for another four months picking up smaller jobs here and there. We let people go to find other work. And oftentimes the payroll would not be covered by what is in the bank account. My friend and I fought about how best to handle this. He continued to spend frivolously at the expense of many people's pay. I finally grew weary of being the nagging partner and I left the company. It was a very hard decision for me because I truly cared about my friend and our company really had potential. I just could not take all the drama anymore.

Not long after that, I began getting the calls, collection calls for the loans we could not pay. I had no extra cash. I was barely making it on my $14 an hour job. I apologized profusely to the creditors. I gave them my friend's number as he was still in business and seemed to be doing just fine financially. They replied with the fact they could not get a hold of him no matter how hard they tried. My hands were tied. The calls kept coming, more frequently and with more threats.

I used what little I had to pay on them, letting personal things fall through the cracks. My income had been cut tremendously, and I ended up having to move from my home and had one of my cars repossessed. Even with that happening, it still wasn't enough to cover the debt I had promised to pay with my business partner. I began trying to reach out to find things to settle these debts. In my research, I discovered that he and I were never actually partners. He had never filed the changes with the state.

Needless to say, I was very hurt and angry. How could someone I trusted deceive me so much? It became my mission to correct the wrongs of this person I had once called friend. The company we had a loan with contacted me and I told them how they could retrieve the trucks and machines we could not pay for. I knew that the amount owed would be lessened by the return of those things. While it did help them, because they had been hidden to keep from repossession, it didn't change the fact I got served papers for default on the loan.

I tried to remain positive. I continued to help the companies get their collateral and equipment or vehicles as I found out where they were. But the thought of a lawsuit of over $198,000 still loomed over my head and consumed my thoughts. I knew there was no way I could repay all that. One day while at work, I got a call from one of the companies. He started out the conversation with, "Melissa, we appreciate the integrity you have shown us in continuing to help when your partner has been hiding. I just got out of a meeting with the president of the company, and he wanted me to contact you. We are dropping you from the lawsuit." I began crying. I was overwhelmed with gratitude. He went on to say, "We are also very aware of how much you have lost personally in this business venture and how much you were deceived. So we want to give you one of our trucks from our fleet. It is an older vehicle we do not need anymore, but we want to bless you with it. All you have to do is title it."

I was speechless! God had honored His word to me. He promises that if we follow Him and obey, He will always take care of what concerns us. He went above and beyond all I could ask or think (also what His word promises).

While the deceit of my friend and the empty promises devastated my heart, there was a silver lining in it all. God had my back. In addition to going from being sued for $198,000 by a company to them giving me one of their vehicles, I found out because the loans had been acquired fraudulently, my liability in all of it was not nearly what it could have been. I had to file bankruptcy. There is nothing more humbling than standing in front of a judge and a room full of people who do not know you and admitting your irresponsible decisions. But I did it. I lost my home, my car, my son's car, and my dignity. But I walked away from the debt that I had agreed to.

I believe God is in the business of taking our faults and failures and turning them into a blessing. He knows our weakness. He is faithful, always. Favor is defined as an act of kindness beyond what is due or usual, and this means unearned. We in our human weakness can earn nothing from God, but it is His free gift to us. And we are so blessed to have One who cares and watches over us even when things look bad, and if we keep going and stay with integrity and honesty and never give up, we cannot help but experience the unending grace and favor of God.

Another time I experienced favor from God was when my husband was released from the military. All through our marriage, I had been a faithful tither. We didn't have much, but I made sure to tithe on all we were given. I went beyond just the tithe. I would give clothing and other household items to anyone and everyone who needed them. My husband did not like me tithing. So I ended up just following God's word on my income alone and not touching his. I knew God would be faithful and see my heart and I would encounter His promises because of it.

He was. And as His word says, "He is not a man that He would lie, And He did all He promised to do."

When it was discovered my husband had violated the military code by having an affair with an underage recruit, it was decided he could no longer stay in service. In all transparency, he could have been dishonorably discharged for this offense, but he wasn't. Instead, in an effort to help him and his family (us), the military decided to demote him to the point where he had to retire. Yes, this affected his retirement pay the rest of his life, but it also allowed him the opportunity to retire honorably. It also gave my children the ability to be covered under military insurance until they graduate college, which was unbelievably helpful especially when I became a single mom. It would have been a much bigger hardship had he been dishonorably discharged than the way they decided to release him from service. I know in my heart God orchestrated this for myself and my children's benefit because I remained faithful in my tithe, offering to Him even in the difficult times.

When favor comes, it is a gift from God. It is not something you can earn. God uses other people to bless you, and there is usually no rhyme or reason to it. There is no "calculation" or "formula" to receive favor; it simply is. Otherwise, it would not be favor. I believe sometimes the people you are receiving favor from cannot even explain why they are doing it, but they just feel led to bless you.

# CHAPTER 6

## *Forgiveness*

LOVE COVERS A MULTITUDE OF sins. What does that even mean? Not only does love—true love—means it protects those in its care, but also it means that when you love someone, it is easy to forgive their faults. Love is sacrifice. Love is selfless. Love is protecting. Love is safe most of all. When someone loves you, truly loves you, you can let your guard down and be you. There are no preconceived ideas of what you should be. Love is simply just love.

I can say I am an expert on love. I may not have many gifts but one for sure that I possess is love. You see, because I have sought it my whole life, I have perfected it. I know how to truly love another. I know how to accept their faults. I may even overlook them when I should address. I know how to give of who I am to encourage, support, and believe in. I carry my heart on my sleeve, and while this makes me an emotional roller coaster at times, interestingly enough it makes me steady as they come. I can let my emotions get the best of me and do or say things that make no sense and seem unstable. Yet I quickly recover, and I refuse to be moved even in my hurt.

One example of this is my husband. Every single affair or lie or misrepresentation I would feel to my core. It would hurt inexplicably. I would run through scenarios in my mind of what I could or should do. Some made complete sense and others were absolutely ridiculous. Regardless of the betrayal and my wild ideas that followed, I would always come to my senses and forgive. Not only did I forgive but also I made a point of letting him know how much I still wanted and accepted him, faults and all. Many would see this as weak. I disagree. You see, it takes more strength and self-reliance to actually swallow the hurt and pain and allow another back in your life than it does to ridicule them and shut them out forever.

It is far easier to walk away, to let go than to fight for something you love. Forgiveness makes the way for miracles. Forgiveness says, "You have wronged me, and yet I still believe in you. I still hope the best for you. I still want to know you." Forgiveness is hard to find these days. Most will try to "even the score" or "pay back" a wrong done to them or shut another out forever. But just as Jesus turned the other cheek to those who struck his face, forgiveness says, "I know what you have done, I feel it. And I give you the opportunity to do it again, but I believe you will choose differently next time."

Think about how amazing that action is, how much freedom you can experience when you can truly do that. Why carry hurt and pain around when you can lay it down and simply begin again? A clean slate. I love the saying "you can't go back and change the beginning, but you can start over and change the ending." Forgiveness requires something from you though. It requires faith in the other. It requires belief. It requires risk, and that is the biggest of all. We as humans like our safety. We like being in control, and having unforgiveness gives you that control. You call the shots. You have the power in your hands, and another is at your mercy. But what do you actually gain? There may be a temporary satisfaction, but in the end, it is just an empty feeling and you end up without that person in your life. You have lost out on what they can bring to your life, or already have. There is loss rather than gain.

Again, we will go to my husband. There is a point where you have to be able to say, "I forgive you. But I cannot allow you to continue hurting me." Forgiveness does not mean you are a doormat. It does not mean you accept abuse. It means that there is an opportunity for change, and when it is obvious that change will not occur, I will forgive you, but I will move on. I do this to maintain who I am, not to hurt you. I believe if someone shows they are truly sorry and can admit their wrong, not be caught in their wrong, there is still hope. If they can own their fault and are willing to try, keep going. However, when they continue in the pattern (and you will see it) and ask forgiveness after being confronted and make empty promises with no action, it is time to set the boundary and move on.

Forgiveness is a fine line. Many abuse it. Many give it only to be hurt again. But the Bible says, "Forgive 70 times 7." God felt it important enough to address how often we would be required to forgive others. But the amazing thing is if you sit back and honestly view your life, ask yourself how many times have you needed forgiveness. I cannot count the times for me. So no matter how much I have forgiven others or how much I have endured, it cannot compare to what I have needed to receive in my life. How humbling! None of us can say we are without fault as much as we would like to.

I had a girl in my life who I was close to that had an affair with my husband. She was naïve and fell easily into his charm. I knew her fairly well, so when all the events unfolded, it was devastating to me. I felt betrayed by her and my husband. I forgave them both and we all moved on. After some time, there was another indiscretion on his part, which is what led to our divorce. About a year passed, and I was at a convention and they said, "Turn around and greet those near you." I did this. And as I turned, I saw her staring me in the face, almost in horror. I did the only thing I knew to do—I wrapped my arms around her, held her close as she shook, and simply said, "I forgive you." She wept. I wept. And it was over. I knew that she knew she was forgiven, and I was free from any hurt in my heart toward her. It probably meant more to me than her!

You see, forgiveness gives you freedom. It breaks the cycle of hurt and pain because when you forgive, truly forgive, you actually feel the pain go away. Sure, you may remember the situation, but it no longer has a hold on you. I speak from experience because to this day, I can be cordial not only to my husband but also the women he had in his life besides me. I know I am better off now than I ever was married, and there is a peace I possess because of my willingness to forgive.

I am not perfect by any stretch of the imagination, but I just know how forgiveness works in my heart and that is what I am sharing. My children know because I have expressed over and over that when they do wrong, while I am disappointed with the action, I can forgive that. I love who they are to me and that means more to me than the hurt they have caused. I know I need forgiveness not only from God but also from others in my life. I hope to sow enough forgiveness and love that I can in return receive that from those whom I value and want to stay in my heart and life. We all need love, forgiveness, and acceptance to be truly fulfilled in this life. It is not possible to receive that which we cannot give, so always be "slow to anger and quick to forgive."

Forgiving yourself can be the hardest of all. This was my biggest struggle. I beat myself up for years for things I had thought I had failed at, until one day I sat down and wrote a letter to myself. Here is what it said,

> Here in all my openness and transparency, I am going to say I am sorry. I am sorry I didn't put you first. I am sorry I didn't see your value. I am sorry I was so hard on you. But most of all, I am sorry I listened to everyone else before hearing the truth of who you really are.
>
> Melissa Michelle Marti, I owe you the same honor and respect I give others. You deserve to be loved. You are worthy. You are strong. And you are enough, just you. You are not a loser because you have encountered bad men and moved on. You are the opposite—you are a warrior. You are a protector. You are a lover of what is good and right. You are beautiful because beauty is within. You are all the things you believe in others and more. Why? Because you see past yourself and help others in their life. You give of who you are to make others happy. You sacrifice your comforts so another may experience a better life. You are far more than you have ever believed. You have only seen yourself superficially, but now your true self is coming out, so embrace it, guard

it, and know that you and your value have been established. Nothing and no one can take that from you. You have to surrender it. Never ever give another the power again to define you.

This life is your story to write, so write it well, Mel. Make history. I believe in you.

I cried profusely as I wrote this letter. I read it over and over until it sunk into my heart. I went from having a head knowledge of forgiveness to having a true heart change. It was an amazing release and, I believe, opened the door for God to move in my life to truly heal me.

# CHAPTER 7

## *Love*

I BELIEVE GOD BRINGS PEOPLE into our lives to fill in where we lack. I lacked a family. I lacked love and acceptance and belonging. God brought me the most amazing people in the most unique way. They became my family. They loved me even when I held them at arm's length. They kept their arms and their hearts open to not only me but also allowed me into their life. They taught me how to open my heart and truly love others as well. I believe God brought them to show me how to be who I was created to be.

I met Ruth and Boaz when I married my husband. They had actually taken him in as their own son. They loved him and believed in him and encouraged him, and he introduced me to them because I believe in his heart, he wanted me to experience that as well. They were (and to this day) an amazing family. He was a doctor who had studied to be a pastor, and she was the epitome of being an amazing mom. They had three children of their own but were always taking in people to stay with them.

I feel they have the gift of not just hospitality where they make you feel welcome but go beyond to show you what love really looks like. In the beginning, I was skeptical; they did not really like me, I told myself. They just wanted to keep my husband in their lives, so they had to tolerate being with me. I was constantly looking for proof of this, only to find none of it had any merit whatsoever. In fact, when our first child was born, they became her nana and papa. They loved her like she was their own.

We all are given gifts from God in who we are. These gifts are not always what I would call an obvious gift. When I met my new family, I believed I had no true gift. They showed me otherwise. They were always supportive and encouraging. They were present in every major and even sometimes minor event of my life. Their constant and steadfast love taught me so much.

I remember Ruth saying to me one day at the very early stage of my marriage, "Love does not keep a marriage together. Marriage keeps love together." What this meant was that the promise of marriage, to be present and not give up, kept love going. Love is an action word; it is not an emotion as we all would like to believe. I took her words to heart. I gave everything in my power to keep love going through my marriage, which is why it was devastating to me to have to tell them I was divorcing the man I promised to love forever.

But I truly did love him, even after it all. My love never wavered. I loved him enough to let him go. I loved myself to protect myself and my children from further hurts. Ruth and Boaz continued to love me even when I felt I let them down. They stayed by my side through it all. And the absolutely amazing thing is they stayed beside my husband as well. They extended to him the same grace, mercy, and compassion they showed me. That is love. The love of the Father shown through man. They always allowed God to work through them in order to bless others. I learned so much from their example and have so much of them in me.

I believe God gave me the spiritual DNA of both Ruth and Boaz. I did not have their physical DNA, but I was intertwined with them forever. They became part of who I am. To this day, my children and I are a very integral part of their lives and they ours. Their love has grown and expanded beyond what I could ever hope for. I am humbled that God set aside such an amazing family for me to a part of. I know what it feels like to be "adopted" as they chose me. They did not just get me from birth, but they literally chose me to be part of their family.

Once I was asked what my gift in life was. Well, thought long and hard about this as I do not have many outwardly visible giftings like singing or acting or creating things. As I thought about it, I realized my gift is the gift of love. I know that it is not of myself, but it is from God. And it was fostered so well by my adopted parents Ruth and Boaz. Let me explain. Matthew 5:46–48 talks about truly loving people.

Yes, I want to be loved, for who I am forever. But love hurts too. When you love someone, you leave your heart open for destruction, and it is dangerous and risky. You expose yourself to rejection, failure, and pain. And because it is so risky, it can be easy to give up. This is what most people do. They never did. And I do not either.

The spirit of God gives me the ability to love those who don't love me back, just as God loved us when we were sinners (Romans 5:8) and Jesus while he was being crucified (Ephesians 2:4–5). Love hurts the lover because love is meant for difficult and cruel people, not just easy and loving people. After all, even non-Christians can love those who love them back. Transactional love is easy give—love gets love.

But true love, the love God asks for, is different altogether. They were unbelievably amazing examples to show me how to give with no expectation of return.

The love commanded by God is more than a feeling, so it is not dependent on what people do or say. We know this because God commands us to love, and you cannot command a person to *feel* something. Because God commands us to love Him, to love others, and to love our enemies, we know He is not commanding a feeling, but an action. This means what drives me to love is God's spirit. To be strong enough to love fearlessly, to love even when not loved in return, or to love in the face of anger or even hate is to truly love another.

The verse I have stood on for years through many relationships is 1 Corinthians 13: "Love is patient, love is kind. It does not envy..., it is not proud, it is not rude, it does not insist on its own way, it is not resentful... It does not rejoice at wrong doing but rejoices in the truth. Love bears all things, believes all things, hopes all things, endures all things. Love never ends."

I am thankful for the love I was gifted with through Ruth and Boaz. I strive to exemplify that same measure to those I meet. I am still a work in progress, but thankfully I am not a hopeless cause.

# CHAPTER 8

## Grace: Integrity Matters

GRACE IS DEFINED AS GOODWILL. I had not experienced much of that in my life. As a matter of fact, even in business, I struggled finding my place. After I left the church, I went to work for my friend's client. The owner claimed he was a Christian man, as many do. What I think most people mistake being a "Christian" for is one who is not Jewish or Muslim, which is not the true definition of a Christian at all. In my heart, being a Christian means I am a follower and I act as He would. This man was anything but that.

In fact, he often ridiculed me, called me names, and even cussed me out. He was not an honest man and I was in charge of his finances. When I would bring things to the other investor's attention about issues, I would get threatened to keep my mouth shut. It was a very precarious position for me. Not long after I started, things began going sideways, and a new owner Brad took over. I was worried, to say the least. I had not seen anything I thought I could stay in long term, and I desperately needed a job to provide for my kids. But he proved me wrong. I believe because I maintained my integrity even when it was not appreciated and often scorned, God gave me a better boss. Brad knew the troubles, he knew the uphill battle that was coming, yet being the man of integrity he is, he took the challenge on full steam ahead. He came in and challenged the entire company to be better, to be more thorough, and to have a commitment to excellence. (He's the kind of guy that notices a misplaced comma and will let you know.) But he doesn't do this out of a need to be critical; he does it because he believes in giving the very best, all the time, every time.

My favorite thing he said to me when we first began working together is, "I will be your biggest fan and your biggest critic in the same conversation if it is warranted." And he has lived up to that statement in every way. I saw him first-hand follow through on a commitment that wasn't even his to begin with. It was refreshing and inspiring to see him find a way to make good on the promise of the former CEO of our company. I learned from Brad that criticism can be good if the intention is to better you and not tear you down. I had been one who could never hear anything without taking it as a personal attack, but I was learning from him, slowly but learning.

When you've been in the business world and watch day after day the dog-eat-dog mentality, you become jaded that there is no one out there who will have your back. You feel like you are totally on your own, but working with Brad, I got a glimpse into what it means to have true integrity. I saw firsthand how he dug into his own pockets to fulfill a monetary promise that he didn't even make, just to help an employee be made whole in their job.

His integrity spreads to those he is around. He surrounds himself with people of like character. "I don't like to be involved with people that don't have the same values. You do your chores before you play. My word and my integrity are sacred. My reputation is important, and I will not allow anyone to tarnish it." He tells how he usually makes the best decisions based off his gut. You don't hear that much anymore. Mostly what is heard is greed, what makes the most money for yourself even if it hurts others. And decisions are made that affect many people's lives based off pride and the need to be on top. But Brad has managed to shut out the voices of greed and pride and has made a habit of listening to his "gut," his instincts.

"All of a sudden, it all made sense. I have always been someone that will take the charge, take the lead, etc., because it's never good enough until I have put in all my effort as well. But when I realized that I serve everyone else, a real sense of purpose set in. That is more of a reason for being here than anything else." Giving of yourself and supporting others is where real success is. He has said to me and to others, "I just need to know you are committed, fearless, responsible, and operate with integrity above all else. If I am loud about something, it means I care." And I can say is I am glad he cares. Because of the grace he showed me, I went on to get my degree finally, and it felt really good.

Having the gift of being able to be mentored by a man like Brad taught me so much. He became a type of father to me. He would not hesitate to correct my mistakes and keep me in line. But he also, challenged me to be better. We have a great working relationship now and I am able to manage my emotions and not take business personally. I have learned a boundary of personal and professional. While we do have our moments of stress, I have learned the balance of it all. He extends grace to me as I grow not only professionally but also in my personal life. They are somewhat a reflection of each other.

Grace is goodwill. And it is out there, and if you give integrity, God will reward you for it.

# CHAPTER 9

## *Lies*

LIES ARE INTENTIONAL. LIES ARE created for many different reasons, such as the fear of being caught or exposed. We lie to avoid trouble or being held accountable for decisions we have made, shame of who we are. We lie because we are wanting to present ourselves differently to be accepted or even lie to spare another person's feelings. Ultimately all lying boils down to personal gain. It is easier for you if you are accepted, no one sees your faults, or another person is not upset with you for being honest with them.

Some people are so good at lying they actually believe what they say and can convince you to believe it as well. I knew a lady who convinced everyone she was in labor for thirty-six hours and gave birth to twin boys but one did not make it. The living son believed his entire life that he was a twin when it was just a story told for empathy she wanted from others.

Some people are good at leaving out important pieces of information and thereby causing you to believe something that is false without actually "lying." But omission of facts is really just lying. I was surrounded by lies for much of my life. I began to question others and their motives because I never truly knew if they were being honest or not. People would tell me what I wanted to hear rather than the truth. This was for many different reasons.

Then there are those who suffer from the lies they choose to believe about themselves that go against what God has said or promised over them. The worst lies, I believe, are the lies we tell ourselves. Lies come to distort our view of ourselves to keep us from living the life God intended for us. We all have struggles and things to deal with as we are human. But where we encounter problems are when we choose to act on the lies that are spoken over us by others or lies we hear in our hearts questioning our value or worth. That is when we become paralyzed in our destiny.

I had been guilty of this. I heard voices in my head telling me I was nothing. They were voices of the past, of those who sought to hurt me. I heard voices of the present telling me how disappointed they were with the way I looked. I heard voices in my head telling me I had no hope, no future, and no one to care. And I chose to believe them, and it caused me to detour on the path God had planned for me. You see, God has already said who we are in Him. Either we can choose to believe it and walk in victory or we can choose to believe others and walk in defeat. Listen to what I said—"in Him" because honestly outside of Him, we really are nothing. We were *not* called to live this life alone. We were called to live it with God.

There is no man, woman, or circumstance that can take the place of the presence of God. Only He can fill that void. We search all over. We try everything. And we sometimes give up because we are not looking for or listening to the One who made us, who loves us, who has a purpose and a destiny set aside from the beginning of time. Only you can fulfill your destiny. There is no one better equipped or more qualified than you. Why? Because it is the calling and destiny He set aside only for you.

He doesn't care what you look like. He doesn't care about your faults. He doesn't see your failures. When God looks at you, all He sees is His creation. And it is perfect, every part. Fat, thin, rich, poor, smart, average—it does not matter. We have to get to the place in our lives where the lies cease and only truth is allowed. That is where freedom is.

# CHAPTER 10

## Healing

"LAUGHTER DOES A HEART GOOD like medicine." There is nothing in this life that has brought me more laughter and fullness than my children. I always wanted to be a mom. It was my biggest dream. And God fulfilled that dream just as He does everything else, exceedingly and abundantly beyond what I could ask or think! I am often in wonder and amazement how He would decide and trust me with the five precious souls He has. There were many days where my children were the only good thing I could see in my life, my only reason for not giving up. It is funny how God uses your children to teach you things about yourself.

Meg, my oldest and definitely strongest of the bunch, was my first and most difficult baby for sure. She had colic the first few months of her life. She taught me that sometimes in life, you can't fix another's issues. They just have to get through it on their own. I remember one day when no matter what I did, she would not stop screaming. I tried everything I knew. So I decided to lie down next to her and just cry with her. We both wore ourselves out and fell asleep.

Meg was an incredibly smart girl. She was reading chapter books at four years old. She could not get enough of them. Her passion for books was so strong that one time I had to punish her, I took all her books out of her room. She was so angry with me she screamed, "I hate you!" I stood on the other side of the door and cried. I never wanted to hear those words from my own child. I took a few moments to let her work out her anger, while I gathered my heart. When I went back into her room, I scooped her in my arms, looked her straight in the face, and said, "It is okay to be angry. But it is never okay to say something you do not mean to hurt another. You cannot take back what has been said. So always pick you words carefully." She buried her head in my chest and sobbed. Again, I sobbed right along beside her.

Meg and I had a unique relationship as she was my first. We were very, very, different in our personalities but very close to each other. There have been many times Meg has encouraged me in my journey both outright and unknowingly. She knew of the trials I experienced with her dad, and she always encouraged me to take care of myself. She had an inner strength unlike any I had seen and a steadfastness in knowing what she wanted and expected from life. Even though things did not always go as she hoped or planned, she would dig her heels in and refuse to give up. She would simply go another way and find her success. She did just that and is now living her dream with my son-in-law, Harry.

Caleb is my seeker of justice and a gentle giant. My children like to have this competition of who they say I love the most. It is endearing to me as I know in my heart, they all know their value to me. Caleb's claim to this being him is that he is the only child I actually asked God for. All the others were a surprise. I did ask for a blond-haired, blue-eyed boy and that is exactly what I got, and so much more. Caleb gets his strong feeling of justice from me. We lovingly refer to him as the "police officer" and ironically that is what he is studying to become.

Not only is he a rule follower, but also he is a rule enforcer. And he has always been. When he was in second grade at a Valentine's Day party, he was so distraught because the other students were not following what the teacher had said to first, color the picture and, second, clean up their desk prior to eating a donut. He could not enjoy the moment because all he could see was the "misconduct" of others (or so he viewed it). Another memory of this was when we went to an ice cream specialty store just recently (Caleb is twenty-one now) and he could not enjoy his ice cream because someone had brought their dog in the restaurant. He knew it was not a service animal, and it was all he could do to not address it with them.

I chuckled, patted him on the leg, and said, "You are ruining the memory because your focus is on others and not us. Relax and focus on you." He rolled his eyes as he often does to me because he thinks I do not understand him, when in all reality, I get where he is coming from. I think everyone should be held to the same rules and standards, and there should be no exceptions. I have just learned over time that you cannot will another to change, or be different, or have the same values as you do. It is far better to just let it go.

Evelyn, my perfectionist (like her momma), strives so hard to be what she believes everyone thinks she should be. Oh, my sweet Evie. She is by far the most like me. I see in her all the weaknesses I struggle with. But I also see in her the strengths I have been given. She has battled fear her entire life. Caleb thought it funny when she was only three years old to tell her if she rode her big wheel over the drain in the basement, it would blow the house up. She believed every word that he said and would take the long way around just to avoid that drain.

Evelyn also struggles with thinking she has to be perfect. She is currently studying animal sciences and has very difficult classes. She got her first less than great score on a test. It was a 69%. She told me she needed to just quit. I reminded her of the things that she had wanted to quit in the past, flag team and her dual education classes. I asked her how it felt to push through and accomplish what she thought was impossible. She hugged me and said that I had forced her to keep going and it helped her believe in herself. She told me most perfectionists are also procrastinators because they would rather not do it at all than get it wrong. Oh, how I know the truth of this statement.

Evelyn is my hardest-working child because things did not come easily for her as they did both Meg and Caleb. School was a challenge. She didn't have the "natural" ability to understand. She would have to study and practice, but this caused her to understand the value of not giving up even when everything in you wants to. She is constantly encouraging me to keep going. She believes there is no one out there good enough for me. I love her heart and how she sees me.

Jacob is my charming affectionate lover of people, accepting anyone and everyone just as they are. Jacob was born on Friday the 13th and has been the sweetest gift of love and affection. When he was little, he would bring his blanket to me and require that we "snuggle just five minutes" as he would so innocently ask. He literally could not start his day until that requirement had been met. Jacob caused me to slow down in life and appreciate just being together.

Now, Jacob keeps me on my toes because he is constantly running and doing and being everywhere and in everything. He is a senior in high school and almost out of the house, and it can't come soon enough for him. He has big dreams and a plan to fulfill those for sure. He loves to perform and is always sharing his new song on the guitar or his new health plan for himself or a friend.

When his dad and I separated, his only concern was that we would both be okay. He is my peacemaker in every way. He could not dream of intentionally causing harm to anyone. In fact, he goes out of his way to be kind and considerate to everyone, always giving them the benefit of the doubt. He encourages me to see the best in others no matter what.

Will is the baby, who is unbelievably brilliant and caring and has the softest heart. Will is what I lovingly refer to as my shock-and-awe baby. I was more than done having children when God decided to bring him into my life. He was so adventurous and unafraid of anything I could hardly believe he was my child. Not only was he a total fireball, but also he was so incredibly smart. If we didn't keep him busy, he would get into all kinds of mischief. I always said he had the face of an angel because God knew he would melt my heart to look in those big brown cow eyes. There were many times Will would mastermind something only to get Jacob in trouble. He had a fiery bold spirit, never afraid of the consequences.

Will has the softest heart of any of my kids. He is definitely stubborn and likes to have the stability of knowing what is coming, having a plan for it, and understanding why it is happening. Will likes order, much like his mom. He likes to do things his own way and does not like change. To this day, he still has the blanket I made for him when he was born. He is sentimental and always considerate.

Harry was brought to our family when he met and married Meg. The best way to describe Harry is a good old country boy. He is great with his hands and he is constantly working. He has been my rock in helping around the house and cars since I have been divorced. He is a strong, young man who is an amazing husband to my daughter. She comments all the time how she does not know how she was so blessed to have him—I just say it was because I prayed. I wanted her to have a better life than I did.

I have learned that children bring healing to your heart. The Bible says they are a blessing from God—"Blessed is the man who has a quiver full." I think I qualify as one of those. There were many times I wondered why I had so many children, but each one has taught me so much. They have been my inspiration, and when I feel I am failing at life and see I did something right, it was being their mom.

# CHAPTER 11

*Hope*

HOPE IS A FEELING OF trust. Wow, this is a big one for me. The only thing I was ever sure of was that life was difficult and everyone would be better off without me. I always wanted to believe the best, but time and again, I was proven wrong. Yet somehow God showed me how to find a new hope.

My younger brother Vinny has a little boy who was diagnosed with leukemia at only nine months. He went into remission for almost two years, and then it was discovered the cancer had returned. Vinny and Emily were devastated. They began treatment again. My nephew had a bone marrow transplant but it did not work. His body rejected it. During this time, Vinny's dad (my stepdad) found out his cancer had spread to other parts of his body. Vinny called me crying.

He said the two most important men in his life and he could lose both. He went on to explain how he couldn't be there for both and wondered if I could help with his dad. This man, my stepdad, and I had a strained relationship but I agreed. Months went by, and both were in hospitals fighting for their lives. Vinny would call me and ask what he should do. I told him, "You have the authority over your son. You pray and you speak over him, every day. Every time the medicine is administered, you declare that it works and his body is healed." There is power in prayer. There is authority given by God to us as His children to change things.

Guess what. One day, I got the call from Vinny and he said, "My son is better. And it is because I did what my big sister said, and I prayed." I wept. My words had impacted him. I don't know why, and I am not sure how, but they mattered. God had used them to help another. And his dad went home from the hospital as well. God had worked a miracle for Vinny, his son, and his father.

Hope means you don't give up. You stand even when circumstances say you shouldn't. Hope is contagious. When you surround yourself with others who believe, you find yourself believing as well.

Not only did He work a miracle for them, but also He gave me the courage to hope and believe again, to step out and share my heart with others, and to know that He can use my words and my heart to others along the way. How humbling. How amazing. How unbelievably blessed!

Yes, life is hard. Yes, trials come. And yes, you can make it through. Not only can you survive, but also you can thrive! Thriving means to live to the fullest, not simply scrape by. Jesus came to give us life and give it abundantly. We have to stay in faith and hope in all things, even the difficult. Success is not living without trials, but success is living through the trials.

I have had many people who know my life circumstances make the comment that they would never have been able to survive. That they would be in a mental institution or severely depressed. But you cannot think that way. You have to be able to see past where you are at this very moment and know that everything can change. My mother in law, a woman I love dearly used to say to me, "This too shall pass Melissa". And she was right. Both good and bad passes and you have to be able to endure both with grace, love, and most of all hope.

# CHAPTER 12

## *Acceptance*

I LOOKED MY ENTIRE LIFE to be accepted, to honestly feel a part of something or someone. I tried everything. I joined Girl Scouts and got kicked out. (For some reason, they did not appreciate me setting the kitchen on fire during our cooking badge!) I was a gymnast for a couple of years. I played on a softball team. I joined the choir in junior high. But my favorite group of people was the journalism team. I loved taking the photos, developing them, and writing stories on my fellow classmates. While I started all these opportunities with the hope of belonging somewhere, it just was not possible. You see, I moved almost every year and never really got to be part of a group of friends or even part of a team for very long. As soon as I got my grounding and feeling good, it would be time to pack up and move. I took it like a champ, stayed positive, and always went to the next place with high hopes of finding a lasting home. I believe to this day it is why I can thrive in unknown situations. I choose to see change as an adventure, not something to fear or dread. My good friend who stayed my friend up until college used to lovingly refer to me as his little nomad.

My family was not really a family, so I definitely did not feel a part of that. Home was never a safe place. And the people in that home were so broken that I think they tried to be a family, but there was just so much competition and comparison they couldn't see past their own insecurities to truly be there for one another. It was every man for himself in survival. My pastor once told me that when you are in survival mode, all you can do is focus on the now. You are unable to see or even hope for the future. People that are merely surviving can never thrive. And even with the best of intentions, you can never truly live or be present for others because you are too focused on yourself.

This is why (in my heart) growing up, I wanted so badly to create my *own* family. They would be, well, what I wanted in life—loved, encouraged, accepted, supported, and challenged to be the very best they could be. They would always know who they were and to Whom they belong. When I was pregnant with Meg, my only prayer for her was that she know who she was. I said that I would rather deal with a spirit of pride than have a child question their worth. I knew they would not be perfect but would always be giving their best to everyone and everything they encountered. I desperately longed to be a part of the "inner circle," a close-knit group of people who were always there for one another no matter what. I felt that was what family was supposed to be, but I just did not see it in my own. Everyone was too focused on themselves to even bother being there for anyone else. This broke my heart. So my dream became a family of my own.

As a mom, I tried every single day to create that environment. I made myself and my heart available to each child by having "date" days with them where it was just one on one and they did not have to compete for my attention. They would pick the event and I would comply. We did some things that cost money and some things that did not. We would alternate as it gets very costly with five kids! I would write notes for them in their lunches or show up with McDonald's happy meals as a surprise. I was supportive in everything they wanted to try, musically or athletically, and I was at every event they were in as much as humanly possible. I remember one night I went to three different schools to see my son wrestle, my daughter perform a flag routine, and my other son sing in a competition. I was even the president of the PTO. It was crazy times for sure. But it was the most rewarding time of my life.

As a wife, I gave up what I wanted to do in order for him to have what he wanted. I didn't really mind at first because I got to know his interests and be a part of what he enjoyed doing. The problem arose when I totally lost who I was as a person in order for him to accept who I was as a person. I was very good at changing my likes and dislikes for another person. You like football? I like football. You like camping? I like camping too! (I use these as examples, but I actually love both) The point I am trying to make is I would become whatever you wanted me to be in order to feel accepted by you. This only works for a while and then you can't possibly change yourself any more to please them.

My husband was very focused on the external aspects of a wife. He wanted a certain look. He did not place as much value on the inner more worthwhile characteristics that truly make a person. He would comment on how I needed to lose weight (just weeks after having a baby) or that I could not attend a military event with him because I did not look good enough. I was constantly trying to change my "look" to gain his approval. I joined gyms, did fad diets, and even dressed a certain way all to be accepted by the one I was spending my life with.

These things broke me down over time. I began to doubt my worth. Acceptance means to be received as adequate or suitable or enough. I never in my life felt that I was accepted by anyone. I know now part of that was my fault. It was my perception of myself, not just the way others treated me. I would often put the expectation on other people who came into my life that they would not or could not truly accept me for who I really was. They didn't stand a chance because I had already decided in my mind that they did not accept me. There is one person in particular that God brought to my life after my divorce. I was meant to learn from knowing him what acceptance looks like in human form.

His name was Simon. Simon means "the listener" and he definitely was. He became a fast friend to me. We spent many nights having conversation in his kitchen. We laughed a lot. We had so much in common it was a little scary to me. Hours would pass and it felt like minutes together. We had similar stories of life, and we even had scars in almost the same places. I felt at home with him unlike any feeling I had before. I did not have to "be" anything with him, but just myself. I couldn't get enough of him or spending time with him. I grew very attached to Simon, too attached.

You know how they say when a person is starving, truly starving, they should start back slow with food and build up the ability to digest again. This is because of a couple of reasons. First, your stomach shrinks so much that eating too much too fast can actually cause it to burst, and second, your stomach can actually reject what you are feeding it because after long periods of no food, it fills up with gas and will push everything back up. I think this is true emotionally as well. I had been starved for acceptance and attention, and well honestly, I did not take anything slow. I wanted it all and I wanted it all now. I couldn't wait and go slow. I couldn't just sit back and enjoy life and the opportunity to know such an amazing person.

I think I allowed my emotional starvation to cause my relationship with him to explode. In my attempt to "fill" myself, I rushed, I pushed, and I created strife. I had to be aggressive. I had to take charge of this situation, because what if he changed his mind? What if he rejected me? What if he decided I had no place in his life? I had already decided eventually he would not accept me and would leave. He would find another he could accept, and it would not be me. I put my preconceived ideas on him. He didn't even stand a chance. There was nothing that he could do because I had already decided for him.

How unfair of me. I took my past hurts and failures out on a man who I know God brought to my life to bless me, and I literally beat him up, emotionally speaking of course, but that is actually worse than physical. Emotions don't heal as quickly and maybe never fully heal at all. The really sad thing is that he was the last person in the world I wanted to hurt. And that made me even angrier at myself.

Simon was always kind, even when I lashed out at him. When we spent time together, it was always amazing. We never argued or fought. It was the times in between where I grew anxious and afraid. I did not have the confidence in myself and who I was that I had actual value to him. I would punish myself and tell him we couldn't be friends, that I didn't deserve him. He would always be who he was, kind and thoughtful, and respect what I said and leave me alone. But I truly did not desire to be alone. I would ask his forgiveness because I missed him terribly, and he would take me back and we would mend again. As soon as I got to a place of letting him back in, I would get scared and run. The cycle went on and on. (It is very similar to the cycle of abuse I not only witnessed as a child but also lived as an adult.) Oh, how terrible it is to live in hurt. But oh, how scary it is to open yourself up to another.

Intimacy, true intimacy, is exposing yourself to another and trusting that they will protect you. I wanted intimacy because I had just not ever experienced it. I had exposed myself in the past only to be shamed and overlooked, forgotten, and left. I could not endure that again, so I had built these walls around myself to prevent that from ever happening again. When Simon entered my world, it was so unexpected and so amazing I could not accept that it would last. That is why I pushed. I would enjoy what I had as fast as I could because I knew at any moment it would be gone. I had never been enough for anyone—not my dad to live, not my mom to be a part of my life, not my husband to not be with other women, and not even my friend who I supported in business and finances. How could he be any different from those?

But he was different, in every way. You see, Simon knew who he was. He had a solid family life. His parents had been married over forty-five years and were still happy. His siblings were all married and happy with families. He was successful in every way, in all the ways that mattered, self-confidence, joy (he could always see the positive in everything, even the bad things), and contentment, which is why he didn't rush into anything. He did not let his circumstances define him. He was the author of his life. Sure, things did not always go as he hoped, but he would simply take the experience, learn from it, and move on to better things. He made the choice to be who he was, and he liked it. He was just fine being alone because he liked who he was. He had accepted himself. These were things I needed to learn from him. These were qualities

I desperately needed in my own life. There was a reason we met.

Most of all, Simon was stable. He was steady and secure. I was drawn to who he was as a person. I wanted to know everything about him, learn from him, and be a part of his life. I essentially wanted everything he had. His life showed me how far off I had been. And I thought after all this time, I had healed. He only showed me how much I had not. But I desperately wanted to! I wanted acceptance, to be viewed as suitable or enough. I think I even used these words often with Simon, accusing him of not seeing me that way, when in all reality it was I who did not believe. I did not accept who I was, so how could anyone else? I was so busy trying to prove myself to others who did not need me to prove anything because they did accept me. Deep down, it was really myself I was trying to prove to that I was enough. I was trying to gain an identity from another person, which you cannot do. Identity has to come from within. I was at war with Melissa.

I set myself and those I love up for failure because I could not believe. I was too afraid. It was easier to live what I knew in the past than to embark on uncharted territory and allow another person to love me, to accept me. It was safer, but it was also very lonely. And it was self-created loneliness. I put Simon in a box—a box I could control—rather than letting him be who he amazingly was and allow myself to enjoy the moment and not know the future. But trust that the future would be okay, because he was meant to be in my life for who he was for however long it lasted. No matter what, Simon was a blessing to me in every way. He was always there to accept me, the good, the bad, and the very, very ugly side of my insecurities.

I learned a very hard but very valuable lesson on acceptance with the gift of Simon in my life. In order for you to feel the acceptance of others, you must first accept yourself. You cannot look to another for validation. And even if they don't see everything in you, as long as you know it for yourself, you cannot be moved. You will be content no matter what. It does not mean it will not hurt, but it will not destroy or define you. I used to get angry at Simon for saying to me to deal with rejection because it happens to everyone. I thought he could never understand the pain of that because he was so amazing. And he had never felt the pain of rejection the way I had. But what I did not see until now is that what made him so amazing was that he did not let another person get to change how he saw himself. All that mattered was *he* accepted who he was.

I love how God brings others into our lives to teach us about ourselves. Simon was one of my favorite gifts and one I wish I still had. I miss the conversations. I wish I had been whole when we met. I wish I could have truly been a lasting part of his life and he mine. But I know he is part of who I am and will always be. He does not define me, but his acceptance of me in all my striving with him and his constant acceptance of himself taught me how to be who I have always wanted to be.

This journey has been a crazy one for sure but has all been God-ordained and every step has been directed by Him. I will continue to learn more about myself and continue to accept things I find unacceptable in me. I look forward to meeting another Simon, and I hope this time I can take what I have learned about life and love and be a blessing, because in it all—the journey to loving myself—I have learned to allow another to love me without boundaries, boxes, or expectations. For the best kind of love is free flowing. It is easy and it is amazing. The joy is in the journey. Love is not a destination, but an adventure to share.

# AFTERWORD

MY JOURNEY HAS BEEN A long and strenuous one at best. It involved much soul searching. There were many times I wanted to give up and I wavered in the belief I would actually make it through. I thought loving myself meant I would look in the mirror and see a different reflection, one I had envisioned in my mind, one that looked nothing like what I currently saw.

I actually would stand in front of the mirror and talk to myself, lecture myself, and even yell at myself for my actions. Eventually, I got to the point where I could encourage myself and believe there was change. It was not a physical change, but it was tangible.

I became more confident in who I was and appreciate my differences from others rather than seeing them as shortcomings. Life is about perspective- when you learn that different does not mean better or worse- just different you can begin to have a healthy perspective. But you have to be the one to decide. No one can do it for you. You are the author of your life. With God's help, it can and will be an amazing story.

Your desire for change has to be stronger than your desire to stay the same.

CPSIA information can be obtained
at www.ICGtesting.com
Printed in the USA
LVHW041420100320
649437LV00007BA/1143